I Can Coo Cookbook

by Sophie Kay

This is a cookbook your child will enjoy, with easy to understand recipes for foods and beverages that are as much fun to prepare as they are to eat. These recipes are presented in a simple, step-by-step format for youngsters to follow (with, of course, just a little help from you!).

Your children will learn the basic terminology and safety rules of good cooking, as well as how to prepare breakfasts, snacks, sandwiches and main dishes for themselves, their family and friends.

There are also recipes for special occasions, such as Halloween, Easter, birthdays and slumber parties. Youngsters will gain a feeling of pride in their accomplishments, for being able to say, "I made it myself," means they are growing up.

We know you will find this helpful, informative and fun cookbook a fitting introduction for your child to the exciting and creative world of cooking.

ISBN 0-89542-935-7 295

CONTENTS

DO'S AND DONT'S IN THE KITCHEN

1. No bumped heads, please! Always close cabinet doors.
2. Sharp knives seen not felt. Always ask an adult to help you if you need to use a sharp knife.
3. Ouch! a burned finger! Remember to use hot pads.
4. Cutting boards are made for cutting — please don't use the counter or tabletop.
5. Use paper towels to wipe up any spill — so nobody slips and falls.
6. Keep your work space neat. You'll find it's easier to work when everything is in order.
7. Always remember to turn off the oven and burners when you are through cooking.
8. Before you start making any recipe, be sure to read it all the way through. Check to see that you have all the ingredients, the right size pots and pans, and then begin.
9. When you are finished cooking, be sure to clean up and put everything back in its proper place.

THE RIGHT MEASURING EQUIPMENT

Dry Measuring Cups They come in a set of 1 cup, ½ cup, ⅓ cup and ¼ cup, and are used to measure dry ingredients. Measure the ingredients level with the top.

Liquid Measuring Cups They have a lip to make it easy to pour. They are used to measure all liquid ingredients.

Measuring Spoons They come in a set of 1 tablespoon, 1 teaspoon, ½ teaspoon, and ¼ teaspoon. When a recipe calls for measuring spoons, take out the whole set.

THE RIGHT WAY TO MEASURE

DRY INGREDIENTS

Brown Sugar If brown sugar is lumpy, sift it before measuring. Pack firmly into standard measuring cup so the sugar holds the shape of the cup when it is turned out.

Flour Lift flour lightly with a spoon into a standard measuring cup, filling the cup heaping full. Then slide the edge of a metal spatula across the top to "level off" the extra flour.

Leavenings and spices Dip dry standard measuring spoon into baking powder or soda or spice. Fill heaping full, then "level off" lightly with the edge of a metal spatula.

LIQUIDS

Milk, water, corn syrup, etc. Place liquid measuring cup on a flat surface (like the countertop) and fill the cup up to the line. Do not hold the cup in your hand as you may tilt it and not get the right amount.

NEVER A FLOP!

1. Measure ingredients properly and accurately using standard measuring cups and spoons.
2. Bake at the temperature specified in the recipe.
3. Use the size pan called for in the recipe.
4. Let ingredients sit at room temperature for a few minutes before using.

MAKE SURE YOU HAVE THE RIGHT PAN

Pan size is usually stamped on the bottom of the pan. If it isn't there, measure the pan. Place a ruler across the center of the top of the pan. Measure from inside one edge to inside the other edge.

COOKING EQUIPMENT

Cake pan Round or square metal pan used for baking cakes.

Candy thermometer A special thermometer which can be attached to a saucepan to tell you the temperature of the ingredients in the pan.

Casserole dish An oven-proof dish used for baking and serving main dishes.

Colander Large metal basket with holes in the bottom used for straining foods.

Cookie sheet Flat rectangular metal sheet without sides used for baking cookies.

Cutting board Wooden or plastic board used to chop or slice food (so tabletop will not get scratched).

Double boiler Pot which has two parts. One pot fits on top of the other. Water is put in the bottom pot and brought to a boil while food is put into the top part to cook.

Egg beater Hand beater used to beat eggs or other foods.

Frying pan A heavy shallow metal pan also called a "skillet." It is used for frying food.

Jelly roll pan A flat rectangular metal baking pan with shallow sides, usually 15 x 10 x 1-inch.

Metal spatula Similar to a knife but has no cutting edge. It has a flexible blade and is used for taking cookies off a cookie sheet, spreading frosting or leveling off dry ingredients.

Mixing bowls Bowls which are used to combine or blend ingredients.

Pancake turner Wide metal spatula with a handle used to turn pancakes or other foods.

Pastry brush A wooden handle with soft bristles like a paint brush.

Pot holders (Hot pads) Cloth pads used to protect your hands when you lift hot pans or utensils.

Rolling pin Wooden or plastic roller with two handles. It is used to roll dough for cookies or pies.

Rubber spatula A flexible rubber blade with a handle. It is usually used to scrape a bowl clean.

Saucepan Pot with a handle used to cook food in.

Sifter Looks like a large metal cup with a screen on the bottom and a special handle. It is used to sift dry ingredients like flour.

Strainer A kitchen tool with a fine wire net used for straining liquid from foods.

Wire rack Metal rack with feet to raise it above the table level. Used to cool cakes, cookies or breads when they come out of the oven.

KITCHEN CHATTER

Bake To cook by dry heat, as in the oven.

Beat To mix very fast with a beater or spoon; makes a mixture smooth.

Blend to gently mix two or more ingredients together until smooth.

Boil To cook liquid over heat until it is bubbling and steaming.

Broil To cook by direct heat as under a broiler.

Brown To cook food in a small amount of fat until it turns brown.

Chop To cut food into small pieces with a knife, chopper or scissors.

Cool To allow baked foods to come to room temperature.

Cream To mix ingredients until soft and fluffy.

Cut-in To mix solid fat like shortening or butter into dry ingredients like flour by chopping with two knives or a pastry blender.

Cut into halves To cut food into two equal parts.

Cut into strips To cut food into long, narrow pieces.

Deep-fat fry To cook food in hot fat that is deep enough to cover the food completely.

Dilute To add liquid to an ingredient to thin it.

Drain To pour the liquid off from solid food.

Feeder cap The knob on the blender cap. It comes off so you can add ingredients while blending.

Fry To cook food in hot fat without water or a cover.

Garnish To decorate food to make it look pretty.

Grease To rub a pan with shortening so food does not stick.

Melt To heat food until it is liquid.

Mix To combine ingredients, usually by stirring.

Pinch Less than $\frac{1}{8}$ teaspoon. It's just a pinch of a dry ingredient taken between your thumb and forefinger.

Preheat To heat the oven to the temperature the recipe calls for before putting in the food.

Shred To cut food such as lettuce into very thin strips or to shred food such as cheese by rubbing it against a grater.

Simmer To cook in liquid over low heat. The liquid should be almost but not quite bubbling.

Slice To cut food crosswise into pieces.

Stir To mix one or more ingredients in a bowl using a wide circular motion until well blended.

Strain To separate the liquid from solid food using a strainer or colander.

BREAKFAST

FUNNY FACE PANCAKES
(Using regular and chocolate pancake batter)

YOU WILL NEED:

griddle
2 medium mixing bowls
liquid and dry measuring cups
measuring spoons
pancake turner

sifter
rubber spatula
wooden spoon
small custard cup
fork

INGREDIENTS:

Regular Pancakes:
  ¾ cup corn meal
1¼ cups pancake mix
  4 teaspoons sugar
  1 egg
1¾ cups milk

STEPS TO FOLLOW:
1. Measure corn meal, pancake mix and sugar into sifter and sift into mixing bowl.
2. Beat egg slightly in custard cup.
3. Add egg and milk to dry ingredients and stir to combine.

INGREDIENTS:

Chocolate Pancakes:
  ¾ cup corn meal
1¼ cups pancake mix
  3 tablespoons cocoa

⅓ cup sugar
  1 egg
1¾ cups milk

BEFORE YOU START: Have adult show you how to use griddle. If electric, preheat griddle to 400°.

STEPS TO FOLLOW:
1. Measure corn meal, pancake mix, cocoa and sugar into sifter and sift into mixing bowl.
2. Beat egg slightly in custard cup.
3. Add egg and milk to dry ingredients and stir to combine.

Continued

To Make Funny Faces:

1. Drizzle some of the chocolate pancake batter from a teaspoon onto the hot griddle to form a face (two eyes and a smile).
2. When bubbles form on the chocolate batter, pour ¼ cup of the regular batter over the face.
3. Turn the entire pancake over when the top of the pancake is covered with bubbles and the edges look dry.
4. Brown the other side, about 1 or 2 minutes.
5. Serve with butter and syrup.

About 20 pancakes

STEP-BY-STEP OMELET

YOU WILL NEED:

medium mixing bowl

fork or wire whisk

measuring spoons

dinner knife

8- or 10-inch omelet pan

pancake turner

dinner plate

INGREDIENTS:

2 eggs

2 tablespoons water

  Dash salt

Dash pepper

1 tablespoon butter

1 slice American cheese

STEPS TO FOLLOW:

1. Mix eggs, water, salt and pepper with fork or whisk just until blended.
2. Heat butter in omelet pan over medium-high heat until butter foams. If you sprinkle a drop of water in the pan it will sizzle. Pour in egg mixture.
3. The mixture will cook at the edges at once. Use a pancake turner, and carefully push the cooked part of the egg (the edges) toward the center.
4. As you push the cooked part to the center, tilt the skillet so the uncooked eggs can get to the bottom of the pan. Slide the pan back and forth over the heat to keep the mixture sliding freely.
5. While the top is still moist and creamy looking, place the slice of American cheese on one half of the side of the omelet. (You could also use chopped cooked ham, vegetables like chopped green pepper, tomato or chopped fresh fruit.) Slip the spatula under one side of the omelet and fold it over the filling.
6. Turn the omelet out of the pan onto a plate.
7. Serve your finished omelet.

1 omelet

HARD-BOILED EGGS

YOU WILL NEED:

small saucepan with lid

INGREDIENTS:

4 eggs

STEPS TO FOLLOW:

1. Carefully place eggs in saucepan.
2. Fill pan with enough water to come at least 1-inch above the eggs.
3. Put saucepan over high heat.
4. When water bubbles, turn off heat.
5. Cover pan and set timer for 20 minutes.
6. When timer rings, set pan in the sink and run cold water over the eggs until they are cool enough to handle.
7. Gently tap cooked eggs to crack shells; peel shell from the eggs.
8. For soft-boiled eggs, follow above directions except let eggs stand only 1 to 4 minutes, depending on how firm you want the eggs.

4 eggs

SANDWICHES

MARTI'S SURPRISE SANDWICHES

YOU WILL NEED:

electric griddle
  or large frying pan
rubber and metal spatulas
liquid and dry
  measuring cups

measuring spoons
large mixing bowl
egg beater
pancake turner

INGREDIENTS:

12 slices white bread
 1 cup creamy peanut butter
 1 cup applesauce
 1 cup pancake mix
2/3 cup milk

 2 eggs
1/2 teaspoon cinnamon
 1 teaspoon vanilla
    Pancake syrup (optional)

BEFORE YOU START: Have adult show you how to use electric griddle. Preheat electric griddle to 375°.

STEPS TO FOLLOW:

1. Spread six slices bread with two tablespoons of the peanut butter and two tablespoons of the applesauce.
2. Cover with remaining bread slices.
3. Combine pancake mix, milk, eggs, cinnamon and vanilla into mixing bowl.
4. Beat well, using egg beater until fairly smooth.
5. Generously butter griddle.
6. Carefully dip each sandwich into pancake batter.
7. Grill on preheated 375° griddle until browned on both sides. (If you do not have an electric griddle or electric frying pan, use a large frying pan and cook over medium heat.)
8. If you like, pour pancake syrup over sandwiches.

6 sandwiches

TUNA BUNWICHES

YOU WILL NEED:

medium mixing bowl
large spoon
rubber spatula
dinner knife

can opener
dry measuring cups
fork

INGREDIENTS:

1 7-ounce can tuna
½ cup mayonnaise
2 hard-boiled
  eggs, chopped
¼ cup sweet
  pickle relish

½ teaspoon salt
6 hamburger buns
  Pinch pepper

BEFORE YOU START: Hard-boil two eggs (see page 8).

STEPS TO FOLLOW:

1. Drain tuna.
2. Place in bowl and flake with a fork.
3. Add mayonnaise, eggs, pickle relish, salt and pepper.
4. Blend together.
5. Divide tuna salad evenly and spread over bottom halves of buns.
6. Cover sandwiches with tops of buns, and serve with potato chips and milk.

6 Bunwiches

Texas Dean

TEXAS DEAN

YOU WILL NEED:

large frying pan
  with cover
wooden spoon
small bowl

measuring spoons
can opener
rubber spatula

INGREDIENTS:

1½ pounds ground beef
  1 16-ounce can tomato
    sauce with onion
  1 tablespoon prepared mustard
  1 tablespoon vinegar
  2 teaspoons chili powder

1 teaspoon salt
  Pinch pepper
1 16-ounce can kidney beans
8 buns

STEPS TO FOLLOW:

1. Place ground beef in frying pan over medium heat.
2. Fry, breaking up the beef with a wooden spoon until meat is lightly browned.
3. Pour off the drippings.
5. Put tomato sauce, mustard, vinegar, chili powder, salt and pepper into a bowl.
6. Mix well and add to ground beef in the frying pan.
7. Stir in kidney beans.
8. Cover and cook over low heat 35 minutes.
9. Serve in buns.

8 servings   **11**

BAKING

ONE-BOWL CHOCOLATE CAKE

YOU WILL NEED:

electric mixer and large bowl
metal and rubber spatulas
wooden spoon
large spoon
measuring spoons
pot holders

2 wire racks
sifter
liquid and dry measuring cups
wooden toothpicks
2 8-inch round cake pans

INGREDIENTS:

1½ cups sifted cake flour
1¼ cups sugar
 ½ cup cocoa
1½ teaspoons baking powder
 ½ teaspoon baking soda
 1 teaspoon salt

⅔ cup vegetable shortening
 1 cup milk
 1 teaspoon vanilla
 2 eggs
 1 can ready-to-spread frosting

BEFORE YOU START: Preheat oven to 350°. Have adult show you how to use electric mixer. Grease and flour 2 8-inch round cake pans.

STEPS TO FOLLOW:

1. Measure flour, sugar, cocoa, baking powder, baking soda and salt into sifter and sift into mixing bowl.
2. Add shortening, ⅔ cup milk and vanilla.
3. Beat 2 minutes on low speed in mixer or 150 strokes by hand. Scrape sides and bottom of the bowl often.
4. Add eggs and the rest of the milk.
5. Beat 2 minutes on low speed in mixer or 300 strokes by hand.
6. Pour into 2 8-inch greased and floured cake pans.
7. Place in preheated 350° oven and set timer for 25 minutes. Test cake with a wooden toothpick stuck in the center of the cake. If it comes out clean, the cake is done.
8. If cake is not done, set timer for another 5 minutes.
9. Remove from oven and place on wire racks to cool 10 minutes.
10. Remove cake from pans and cool completely on racks.
11. Frost with ready-to-spread frosting.

1 Chocolate Cake

BUTTERFLY BANANA CAKE

YOU WILL NEED:
electric mixer and large bowl
sifter
metal and rubber spatulas
liquid and dry measuring cups
measuring spoons
pot holders

wire racks
small mixing bowl
fork
wooden toothpick
large spoon

INGREDIENTS:
1½ cups sifted
   all-purpose flour
 2 teaspoons baking powder
¾ teaspoon baking soda
 1 teaspoon salt
1¼ cups sugar
1¼ cups mashed ripe banana
   (about 3 medium bananas)
¾ cup (1½ sticks) softened
   butter or margarine

⅔ cup buttermilk
 2 eggs
1¼ cups quick or
   old-fashioned oats
 1 7-ounce package fluffy
   white frosting mix
   Few drops red food coloring
 3 peppermint candy sticks
   Colored sugar sprinkles

BEFORE YOU START: Preheat oven to 350°. Have adult show you how to use electric mixer. Grease and flour 2 eight-inch round cake pans.

STEPS TO FOLLOW:
1. Measure flour, baking powder, soda, salt and sugar. Sift into large mixer bowl.
2. Mash bananas using fork
3. Add banana, butter and ⅓ cup of the buttermilk to the flour mixture.
4. Beat 2 minutes on medium speed of the mixer. Scrape sides and bottom of the bowl often.
5. Add the rest of the buttermilk and eggs and beat 2 more minutes.
6. Stir in oats and blend well.
7. Pour into 2 eight-inch greased and floured cake pans.
8. Place in preheated 350° oven for 35 minutes. Then stick a wooden toothpick in the center of the cake. If it comes out clean, the cake is done.
9. If cake is not ready, set timer for another 5 minutes.
10. Remove from oven and place pans on wire racks to cool 10 minutes.
11. Remove from pans and cool completely on racks.

To Decorate Cake:
1. Prepare frosting mix following the package directions, adding a few drops red food coloring to make the frosting pink.
2. To make the butterfly shape: Frost top of one layer of cake with a small amount of frosting.
3. Place the second layer on top.
4. Cut the cake in half.
5. Turn each half around, placing curved edges together.
6. Frost all sides and the top of the cake.
7. Insert a peppermint candy stick into each half of the cake for antennae.
8. Lay one peppermint candy stick down the center of the cake for the body.
9. Sprinkle colored sugar over the "butterfly."

1 Butterfly Cake

ROBBIE'S KITTY KATS

YOU WILL NEED:

large and medium mixing bowls
small saucepan
wooden spoon
dry measuring cups
metal and rubber spatulas
large metal spoon
pot holders
sifter

ruler
rolling pin
2 sheets waxed paper
    (10 inches each)
2 cookie sheets
2 wire racks
dinner knife

INGREDIENTS:

2 1-ounce squares
    unsweetened chocolate
2¼ cups all-purpose flour
¾ teaspoon baking powder
½ teaspoon salt
½ cup (1 stick) softened
    butter or margarine
¼ cup shortening

1 cup sugar
2 eggs
1 teaspoon vanilla
1 cup quick or
    old-fashioned oats
Raisins
Black shoestring licorice

BEFORE YOU START: Preheat oven to 350°.

STEPS TO FOLLOW:

1. Place chocolate in small saucepan and melt, using very low heat. Set aside to cool.
2. Measure flour, baking powder and salt into a sifter and sift into medium mixing bowl.
3. Place butter and shortening in large mixing bowl.
4. Beat until smooth and creamy using a wooden spoon.
5. Add sugar and beat until light and fluffy.
6. Add eggs and vanilla and mix well.
7. Add sifted dry ingredients to the creamed mixture and blend well.
8. Stir in oats and mix well.
9. Divide dough in half and add cooled chocolate to one half of the dough.
10. Stir until blended.
11. Shape vanilla dough in the form of a log, 8 inches long.
12. Using a rolling pin, roll out chocolate dough between the two sheets of waxed paper to form an 8-inch square.
13. Remove the top sheet of waxed paper.
14. Place the vanilla log on the chocolate dough and wrap the chocolate dough around the vanilla log.
15. Wrap log in waxed paper and place in the refrigerator until firm — about 3 hours.

Continued

Butterfly Banana Cake, 13
Robbie's Kitty Kats, 14
Surprise Cookies, 16

TO FORM THE COOKIES:

1. Cut the chilled dough into slices about ¼ inch thick.
2. Place each cookie on an ungreased cookie sheet about 1 inch apart.
3. Pinch each side of cookie top to form the ears.
4. Make eyes and whiskers with raisins and licorice (just as in the picture).
5. Place in preheated 350° oven. Set timer for 12 minutes. Cookies are done when they are lightly browned.
6. Remove from the oven and place cookie sheet on rack. Cool slightly.
7. Then remove cookies from the cookie sheet and let cool completely on wire rack.
8. Continue until all cookies are baked.

2½ dozen Kitty Kats

SURPRISE COOKIES

YOU WILL NEED:

large and medium mixing bowls
sifter
wooden spoon
dry measuring cups
measuring spoons
pancake turner

large spoon
metal and rubber spatula
2 cookie sheets
pot holders
wire rack

INGREDIENTS:

2½ cups sifted
   all-purpose flour
¾ cup cornmeal
1 teaspoon baking soda
½ teaspoon salt
1 cup softened butter
  or margarine
1 cup granulated sugar

½ cup firmly packed
  brown sugar
2 eggs
1 teaspoon vanilla
  Jelly beans, candy mints
1 4-ounce tube red
  decorator's icing

BEFORE YOU START: Preheat oven to 375°.

STEPS TO FOLLOW:

1. Measure flour, cornmeal, soda and salt into a sifter and sift into medium-size bowl.
2. Place butter in large bowl and beat with wooden spoon until creamy.
3. Gradually add both sugars to butter and mix until light and fluffy.
4. Add eggs and vanilla to butter mixture and beat well.
5. Add the sifted dry ingredients a little at a time, mixing well.
6. Cover dough with plastic wrap and place in the refrigerator 2 to 3 hours.
7. To form cookies, mold a rounded teaspoonful of dough around each jelly bean or candy mint.
8. Place dough 2 inches apart on a cookie sheet.
9. Place in a preheated 375° oven for 9 to 12 minutes. (Be careful not to burn the cookies.)
10. Remove from the oven. Place cookie sheet on rack and let cool slightly.
11. Then remove cookies from cookie sheet and let cool completely on wire rack.
12. Continue until all cookies are baked.
13. Serve when cool or decorate with red decorator's icing.

5 to 5½ dozen cookies

SNACKS

CARAMEL CORN

YOU WILL NEED:

2-quart saucepan
2 wooden spoons
liquid and dry measuring cups
measuring spoons

jelly roll pan
large mixing bowl
pot holders
tightly covered container

INGREDIENTS:

1 recipe Popped Corn
½ cup peanuts
½ cup (1 stick) butter
   or margarine
1 cup firmly packed light
   brown sugar

¼ cup light or dark
   corn syrup
½ teaspoon salt
¼ teaspoon baking soda
½ teaspoon vanilla

BEFORE YOU START: Make 1 recipe Popped Corn (page 18). Preheat oven to 250°.

STEPS TO FOLLOW:

1. Mix together Popped Corn and peanuts.
2. Add butter to 2-quart saucepan.
3. Place saucepan over medium heat; melt butter.
4. Stir in brown sugar, corn syrup and salt.
5. Bring mixture to a boil, stirring constantly with a wooden spoon.
6. When mixture begins to boil, set timer for 5 minutes and boil without stirring.
7. Remove from heat and stir in soda and vanilla.
8. Pour syrup over Popped Corn and peanuts and mix well.
9. Spread in jelly roll pan.
10. Place in preheated 250° oven and set timer for 1 hour.
11. Stir every 15 minutes.
12. Remove from oven and cool completely.
13. Break apart and store in tightly covered container.

About 5 cups

17

PEANUTTY POPCORN BARS

YOU WILL NEED:

1-quart saucepan
2-quart saucepan
2 wooden spoons
candy thermometer

large mixing bowl
rubber spatula
liquid and dry measuring cups
measuring spoons

INGREDIENTS:

1 recipe Popped Corn
½ cup (1 stick) butter
1 cup firmly packed
   light brown sugar
¼ cup light corn syrup

¼ cup water
1 teaspoon salt
1 7-ounce milk chocolate bar
1 cup chunky peanut butter
   Whole peanuts

BEFORE YOU START: Make 1 recipe Popped Corn (below). Butter one jelly roll pan (15 x 10 x 1-inch).

STEPS TO FOLLOW:

1. Place Popped Corn in large mixing bowl and set aside.
2. Melt butter in 2-quart saucepan over medium heat.
3. Stir in sugar, corn syrup, water and salt.
4. Have adult attach candy thermometer to the saucepan.
5. Cook over medium heat, stirring constantly with a wooden spoon.
6. Continue cooking and stirring until the sugar is melted and the mixture starts to boil.
7. Boil mixture until the thermometer reaches 250°.
8. *Slowly* pour mixture over popcorn.
9. Stir until popcorn is evenly coated with the mixture.
10. Place popcorn mixture into buttered jelly roll pan, pressing down firmly.
11. Melt the chocolate bar and peanut butter together in the 1-quart saucepan over low heat.
12. Stir with wooden spoon until chocolate is melted.
13. Using the rubber spatula, spread chocolate mixture evenly over the popcorn.
14. Let cool until firm and set.
15. Have adult cut into 50 (3 x 1-inch) bars.
16. Place a whole peanut on top of each bar.

About 50 bars

POPPED CORN

YOU WILL NEED:

heavy 4-quart saucepan with lid
measuring spoons
large bowl
small saucepan
2 wooden spoons

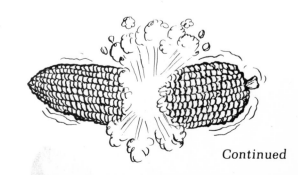

Continued

Caramel Corn, 17
Peanutty Popcorn Bars, 18
Pink Popcorn Balls, 20
Peanut Butter Malt, 21
Strawberry Milk Shake, 20

INGREDIENTS:

3 tablespoons corn oil
½ cup popcorn
¼ cup melted butter
½ teaspoon salt

STEPS TO FOLLOW:

1. Measure oil into saucepan.
2. Add 1 kernel popcorn and place over medium-high heat.
3. When kernel pops, remove it with long-handled spoon and add the ½ cup popcorn.
4. Stir to mix popcorn and oil.
5. Cover pan.
6. Shake the pan every so often until the popping stops.
7. Remove the pan from heat.
8. Add the melted butter and toss well.
9. Sprinkle with salt and toss again.
10. Pour into a bowl and serve.

About 3 quarts

PINK POPCORN BALLS

YOU WILL NEED:

2-quart saucepan
liquid and dry measuring cups
measuring spoons
wooden spoon

fork
small plastic bags
with twist ties

INGREDIENTS:

1 recipe Popped Corn
1 cup light corn syrup
1 cup sugar
½ teaspoon salt

1 teaspoon vanilla
¼ teaspoon red food coloring
Butter

BEFORE YOU START: Make 1 recipe Popped Corn (page 18). Preheat oven to 250°.

STEPS TO FOLLOW:

1. Keep Popped Corn warm in 250° oven.
2. Measure corn syrup, sugar and salt in 2-quart saucepan.
3. Place over medium heat and cook until mixture comes to a boil, stirring constantly using a wooden spoon.
4. When mixture comes to a boil, set timer for 4 minutes and boil without stirring.
5. Remove from heat and stir in vanilla and food coloring.
6. Butter a fork.
7. Pour syrup slowly over Popped Corn, mixing with the buttered fork.
8. Toss the Popped Corn to coat evenly with the syrup.
9. When Popped Corn is cool enough to handle, but still warm, shape into popcorn balls, about 2½ inches wide. (You can make about 10 balls.)
10. Let balls stand until cool so they will lose their stickiness.
11. To store, place popcorn balls in small plastic bags and tightly close, or put in a tightly covered container.

10 popcorn balls

STRAWBERRY MILK SHAKE

YOU WILL NEED:

glass measuring cup
measuring spoons
blender or egg beater

ice-cream scoop
rubber spatula
tall drinking glass

INGREDIENTS:

1 cup milk
3 tablespoons strawberry preserves
1 scoop vanilla ice cream

BEFORE YOU START: Have adult show you how to use electric blender.

STEPS TO FOLLOW:

1. Measure milk, strawberry preserves and ice cream into blender.
2. Cover and blend at medium speed 1 minute. (If you do not have a blender, place ingredients in a bowl and let ice cream soften. Beat well with an egg beater.)
3. Pour into glass and serve immediately.

1 serving

CHERIE'S APPLE CLOWNS

YOU WILL NEED:
round wooden toothpicks
colored construction paper
transparent tape
scissors

INGREDIENTS:
 6 red delicious apples
30 marshmallows
   Green grapes
   Chocolate chips

STEPS TO FOLLOW:
1. Wash apples and remove stems.
2. Put one marshmallow on a toothpick and stick the toothpick into the top of the apple to make the "head."
3. Put a marshmallow and then a grape on a toothpick for each arm and leg and stick them into the apple.
4. To make each hat, cut a 3-inch square of construction paper and wrap it into a cone shape.
5. Hold hat together with tape and place on top of the marshmallow head.
6. Break six toothpicks in half.
7. Attach chocolate chips with the toothpicks broken in halves for eyes, nose, and buttons down the front.

6 Apple Clowns

PEANUT BUTTER MALT

YOU WILL NEED:
electric blender
liquid and dry measuring cups
measuring spoons
ice-cream scoop
rubber spatula

INGREDIENTS:
¼ cup milk
¼ cup maple syrup
¼ cup peanut butter
 1 tablespoon malt powder
 3 scoops vanilla ice cream

BEFORE YOU START: Have adult show you how to use electric blender.

STEPS TO FOLLOW:
1. Put milk, maple syrup, peanut butter, malt powder and ice cream into blender.
2. Place cover on blender.
3. Blend on medium speed one minute. (If you do not have a blender, place ingredients into a bowl. Let ice cream soften, and beat well with electric mixer.)

One 12-ounce serving

MAIN DISHES

CORN DOGS

YOU WILL NEED:

deep fat fryer
sifter
medium-sized mixing bowl
egg beater
pie pan
liquid and dry measuring cups

measuring spoons
paper toweling
tongs
8 wooden skewers (get from the meat
department at the grocery store)
small custard cup
fork

INGREDIENTS:

½ cup cornmeal
½ cup all-purpose flour
1 teaspoon paprika
1 teaspoon salt
½ teaspoon pepper

1 egg
½ cup milk
2 tablespoons vegetable oil
8 frankfurters
Extra flour

BEFORE YOU START: Ask adult to deep fat fry corn dogs for you when you have made them. Place shortening in deep fat fryer and set at 375°.

STEPS TO FOLLOW:

1. Measure cornmeal, flour, paprika, salt, and pepper into sifter and sift into mixing bowl.
2. Beat egg slightly in a custard cup.
3. Add egg, milk, and oil to dry ingredients.
4. Beat with egg beater until smooth.
5. Lightly roll each frankfurter in the extra flour.
6. Then dip each one in the batter to coat evenly.
7. Drain off excess batter.
8. Have adult fry corn dogs in hot, deep fat for 2 to 3 minutes or until golden brown.
9. Remove with tongs and drain on paper toweling.
10. Insert a wooden skewer in each corn dog.
11. Serve with mustard and catsup.

8 Corn Dogs

Pictured Opposite
Frankfurter Casserole, 24

FRANKFURTER CASSEROLE

YOU WILL NEED:

2-quart casserole	tongs
pot holders	paper toweling
rubber spatula	cutting board
measuring spoons	knife
small frying pan	can opener

INGREDIENTS:

4 slices bacon
1 10¾-ounce can condensed cream of mushroom soup
1 tablespoon instant minced onion
½ teaspoon salt
1 8-ounce can peas, drained
1 16-ounce can whole kernel corn, drained
1 15-ounce can sliced potatoes, drained
6 frankfurters, sliced crosswise

BEFORE YOU START: Preheat oven to 350°. Have adult help you slice frankfurters into coins and slice bacon into ½-inch pieces.

STEPS TO FOLLOW:
1. Place bacon pieces in small frying pan.
2. Fry over medium heat until crisp.
3. Remove bacon and place on paper toweling to drain. Set aside.
4. Place soup, onion, and salt in 2-quart casserole.
5. Stir in peas, corn, potatoes and sliced frankfurters.
6. Sprinkle bacon over the top.
7. Place in preheated 350° oven and set timer for 45 minutes.

6 servings

BARBECUED CHICKEN DRUMSTICKS

YOU WILL NEED:

small saucepan	large, shallow baking pan
pastry brush	tongs
measuring spoons	pot holders
liquid measuring cup	wire rack

INGREDIENTS:

2 tablespoons butter or margarine
1 teaspoon salt
8 chicken drumsticks
1 cup barbecue sauce

STEPS TO FOLLOW:
1. Place butter in small saucepan over low heat to melt.
2. Remove from heat and stir in salt.
3. Brush drumsticks with melted butter.
4. Place drumsticks in large baking pan.
5. Place pan in 375° oven and set timer for 35 minutes.
6. Remove pan from the oven and set on top of the wire rack.
7. Pour barbecue sauce over the drumsticks, making sure you cover all of them.
8. Put back into the oven and set the timer for 15 more minutes.

4 servings

BEEF TACOS

YOU WILL NEED:

8 or 10-inch frying pan
wooden spoon
knife

liquid measuring cup
measuring spoons
cutting board

INGREDIENTS:

½ pound ground beef
 1 small onion, chopped
½ teaspoon salt
½ cup taco sauce
 8 taco shells

½ cup shredded
  cheddar cheese
1 cup shredded lettuce
1 large tomato, chopped

BEFORE YOU START: Have adult help you chop the onion and tomato and cut the lettuce into strips.

STEPS TO FOLLOW:

1. Place meat and onion into frying pan. Fry over medium heat until the meat is brown. Use a wooden spoon to help break up the meat and stir it occasionally.
2. Ask adult to help you drain off the fat.
3. After meat is browned, stir in salt and taco sauce.
4. Cook over low heat for about 15 minutes or until all the liquid is gone.
5. To serve: Place about 2 tablespoons meat mixture into taco shell.
6. Top with about 1 tablespoon shredded cheese, then with lettuce and tomato.
7. Serve with additional taco sauce if you like.

8 Beef Tacos

FISHERMAN'S SANDWICH

YOU WILL NEED:

shallow baking pan
medium mixing bowl
dry measuring cups
measuring spoons
rubber spatula

grater
knife
cutting board
pot holders

INGREDIENTS:

 6 frozen, breaded
   pre-cooked fish portions
1¼ cups shredded
   American cheese
 3 tablespoons salad dressing

1 tablespoon sweet
  pickle relish
1½ teaspoons prepared mustard
 6 hamburger buns
1 cup shredded lettuce

BEFORE YOU START: Have adult cut lettuce into fine strips for you.

STEPS TO FOLLOW:

1. Bake fish portions following package directions.
2. Measure American cheese, salad dressing, sweet pickle relish and prepared mustard into bowl and blend.
3. Spread about 2 tablespoons mixture on each fish portion during the last few minutes of baking time.
4. Heat just until the cheese is melted.
5. Serve each fish portion on a bun with shredded lettuce.

6 sandwiches

Lime Float
Backyard Coney, 28
Carousel Cutouts, 28
Deviled Eggs, 27
Vegetable Dipper, 27

LIME FLOAT

YOU WILL NEED:
2-quart pitcher
ice-cream scoop
4 tall drinking glasses

INGREDIENTS:
1 6-ounce can frozen lemonade
1 10-ounce bottle sparkling water, chilled
1 pint lime sherbet

STEPS TO FOLLOW:
1. Place frozen lemonade in pitcher.
2. Add 3 cans water.
3. Pour in sparkling water and stir.
4. Put scoops of lime sherbet in the bottom of 4 tall glasses.
5. Pour in sparkling lemonade mixture and serve immediately.

4 servings

BIRTHDAY PARTY

DEVILED EGGS

YOU WILL NEED:
dinner knife
teaspoon
fork
rubber spatula
small bowl

INGREDIENTS:

4 hard-boiled eggs
1¼ teaspoon prepared mustard
¼ teaspoon salt

Pinch pepper
3 tablespoons mayonnaise
Parsley for garnish

BEFORE YOU START: Hard-boil 4 eggs (see page 8).

STEPS TO FOLLOW:
1. Peel the eggs. Cut them in half lengthwise with dinner knife.
2. With a spoon, remove the yolks from the egg halves.
3. Mash the yolks with a fork.
4. Add the mustard, salt, pepper and mayonnaise.
5. Mix well.
6. Refill the egg whites.
7. Garnish with parsley.

8 stuffed egg halves

VEGETABLE DIPPER

YOU WILL NEED:
medium mixing bowl
dry measuring cups
measuring spoons
rubber spatula

INGREDIENTS:
2 cups sour cream
1 tablespoon lemon juice
1½ teaspoons dill weed
½ teaspoon salt

STEPS TO FOLLOW:
1. Measure all ingredients into the mixing bowl.
2. Blend well and chill in the refrigerator at least 1 hour.
3. Serve with fresh, crisp vegetables or chips.

About 2 cups

BACKYARD CONEY

YOU WILL NEED:

frying pan with cover
wooden spoon
can opener
measuring spoons
dry and liquid measuring cups
large spoon

wooden toothpicks
fork
knife
cutting board
saucepan
tongs

INGREDIENTS:

½ pound ground beef
1 small onion, chopped
1 6-ounce can tomato paste
1⅔ cups water
¾ teaspoon salt
½ teaspoon chili powder
⅛ teaspoon oregano

¾ cup drained kidney beans
1 loaf French bread
   cut in half lengthwise
1¼ cups shredded lettuce
4 hot dogs
2 slices American cheese

BEFORE YOU START: Have adult chop onion, cut bread in half lengthwise, and cut lettuce in thin strips.

STEPS TO FOLLOW:

1. Put meat and onion in frying pan. Fry over medium heat until brown. Stir often with a wooden spoon to break up the meat.
2. Add tomato paste, ⅔ cup water, salt, chili powder and oregano.
3. Stir to mix well.
4. Cover and simmer over low heat for 20 minutes.
5. Stir in beans. Cover and cook 10 more minutes.
6. While this is cooking, put 1 cup water in saucepan and bring to a boil over high heat.
7. Using tongs, place hot dogs into the boiling water and cook to heat through, about 3 minutes.
8. Remove from heat and set aside.
9. Remove meat mixture from heat and spoon over the bottom half of the bread.
10. Place shredded lettuce over meat and top with hot dogs.
11. Fold each slice of American cheese and break into 4 triangles.
12. Place a cheese triangle over top of each hot dog. Cover with top half of bread.
13. Fasten sandwich with toothpicks before cutting into 4 pieces.

4 servings

CAROUSEL CUTOUTS

YOU WILL NEED:

medium and large
   mixing bowls
wooden spoon
liquid and dry
   measuring cups
measuring spoons
metal and rubber spatulas

2 cookie sheets
3 to 4-inch animal
   cookie cutters
wire rack
pot holders
cutting board
rolling pin

Continued

INGREDIENTS:

½ cup (1 stick) softened butter   ¾ teaspoon baking soda
½ cup sugar   1 teaspoon ginger
1 egg   ½ teaspoon cinnamon
⅓ cup molasses   ½ teaspoon cloves
1 tablespoon vinegar   ¼ teaspoon salt
2¼ cups all-purpose flour   Vanilla Icing

BEFORE YOU START: Preheat oven to 375°.

STEPS TO FOLLOW:
1. Measure butter and sugar into large mixing bowl.
2. Use wooden spoon and cream until light and fluffy.
3. Add egg, molasses and vinegar and beat until well blended.
4. Measure flour, soda, ginger, cinnamon, cloves and salt into medium mixing bowl. Stir to mix ingredients.
5. Slowly add the dry flour mixture to the creamed butter mixture and mix well.
6. Cover bowl with plastic wrap and place in the refrigerator to chill, at least 1 hour.
7. Divide dough into thirds.
8. Lightly sprinkle some flour on a large cutting board or the tabletop.
9. Roll out the dough to ⅛-inch thickness.
10. Cut with assorted animal cookie cutters.
11. Place cookies on cookie sheet about 1 inch apart.
12. Place in preheated 375° oven 7 to 9 minutes, or until cookies are very lightly browned.
13. While cookies are baking, roll out the remaining dough.
14. Remove from the oven and place on rack to cool slightly. Then remove the cookies from the cookie sheet and let cool completely on the rack. Continue until all cookies are baked.
15. Use a metal spatula and put Vanilla Icing on the cookies.(It is important to let the icing dry thoroughly before decorating the cookies.) To decorate the cookies, paint with food colors as in the picture (page 26).

About 4 dozen cookies

VANILLA ICING

YOU WILL NEED:
dry measuring cups
measuring spoons
medium mixing bowl
wooden spoon

INGREDIENTS:
1½ cups confectioners' sugar
½ teaspoon vanilla
2½ tablespoons milk

STEPS TO FOLLOW:
1. Measure sugar, vanilla and milk into mixing bowl.
2. Mix well to blend all ingredients.
3. If icing is too thick, stir in a teaspoon of milk.

Party Cocoa
Bologna Cups, 32
Chocolate Chip Cookies, 31

PARTY COCOA

YOU WILL NEED:
2-quart saucepan
liquid and dry measuring cups
wooden spoon

INGREDIENTS:
$\frac{1}{3}$ cup cocoa

$\frac{1}{4}$ cup sugar

  Pinch salt

$\frac{1}{2}$ cup water

4 cups (1 quart) milk

6 marshmallows

STEPS TO FOLLOW:
1. Measure cocoa, sugar, salt and water into saucepan.
2. Bring to a boil over medium heat.
3. Boil 2 minutes, stirring constantly.
4. Then pour in milk and heat again. *Do not boil.*
5. Pour into cups and top with a marshmallow before serving.

6 servings

FOOTBALL PARTY

CHOCOLATE-CHIP COOKIES

YOU WILL NEED:

small and large
  mixing bowls
dry measuring cups
measuring spoons
sifter
rubber and metal spatulas

wooden spoon
wire racks
teaspoon
pot holders
large spoon

INGREDIENTS:

1 cup all-purpose flour
½ teaspoon baking soda
½ teaspoon salt
½ cup (1 stick) softened
  butter or margarine
6 tablespoons granulated sugar

¼ cup firmly packed
  brown sugar
1 egg
½ cup chopped nuts
1 6-ounce package semi-
  sweet chocolate chips
1 teaspoon vanilla

BEFORE YOU START: Preheat oven to 375°.

STEPS TO FOLLOW:

1. Measure flour, soda and salt into a sifter and sift into a small bowl. Set aside.
2. Place butter in a large mixing bowl and cream with a wooden spoon.
3. Add both sugars and cream until fluffy.
4. Beat in egg.
5. Stir in flour mixture.
6. Mix in nuts, chocolate chips and vanilla.
7. Drop from rounded teaspoons on cookie sheet about 2 inches apart.
8. Place in preheated 375° oven for 10 to 12 minutes or until cookies are lightly browned.
9. Remove from the oven. Place cookie sheet on a rack and let cool slightly.
10. Then remove cookies from the cookie sheet and let cool completely on wire rack.
11. Continue until all cookies are baked.

3½ dozen cookies

BOLOGNA CUPS

YOU WILL NEED:

large frying pan
paring knife
cutting board
tongs
medium mixing bowl
egg beater

liquid measuring cup
measuring spoons
small saucepan
2 large spoons
can opener
large platter

INGREDIENTS:

1 16-ounce can German-
   style potato salad
2 tablespoons butter
   or margarine
8 slices bologna

4 eggs
¼ cup milk
¼ teaspoon salt
2 or 3 radishes

BEFORE YOU START: Have adult help you slice 2 or 3 radishes.

STEPS TO FOLLOW:

1. Put potato salad into saucepan and place over medium heat until hot.
2. Turn heat to low to keep potato salad warm.
3. Melt butter in frying pan over medium heat.
4. Add bologna slices and brown both sides, using tongs to turn. (As the bologna heats it will curl to form cups.)
5. Remove bologna from the pan, using the tongs, and set aside.
6. Put eggs, milk and salt into bowl and beat with egg beater
7. Pour egg mixture into the frying pan. Cook eggs over low heat until eggs are solid. Stir once in a while.
8. Place 4 bologna cups on large platter and fill cups with scrambled eggs.
9. Fill the other 4 bologna cups with the hot potato salad.
10. Arrange radish slices on top to decorate.

8 bologna cups

NUTTY COCOA

YOU WILL NEED:

liquid and dry measuring cups
2-quart saucepan
rubber spatula
wooden spoon

INGREDIENTS:

⅓ cup cocoa
½ cup sugar
   Pinch salt
4 cups (1 quart) milk
1 cup peanut butter

STEPS TO FOLLOW:

1. Measure cocoa, sugar and salt into saucepan.
2. Blend in ¼ cup of the milk and the peanut butter.
3. Stir in the rest of the milk and heat over medium heat. *Do not boil.*
4. Serve hot; or place in the refrigerator to chill and serve cold.

5½ cups

HALLOWEEN PARTY

HOBGOBLIN BURGERS

YOU WILL NEED:

wooden spoon
measuring spoons
broiler pan
wooden toothpicks
pancake turner

hot pads
wire rack
knife
cutting board
dinner knife

INGREDIENTS:

1½ pounds ground beef
6 slices American cheese
6 lettuce leaves
6 hamburger buns, split
1 tomato, cut into 6 slices
18 sweet pickle slices

12 pimiento slices
12 dried apricot halves
12 raisins
3 radishes, cut in half
3 midget gherkins,
    cut in half lengthwise

BEFORE YOU START: Have adult help you slice the tomato and cut radishes in half and then into diamond shapes.

STEPS TO FOLLOW:
1. Shape beef into 12 patties, each 4 inches round.
2. Place 1 slice of cheese on top of each of the 6 patties.
3. Top cheese with the rest of the 6 patties.
4. Pinch the edges very well to seal.
5. Place on the broiler pan.
6. Ask adult to help you adjust the oven racks so the surface of the meat is 4 inches from the source of the heat.
7. Ask adult to help you turn on the broiler.
8. Place pan under the broiler and set the timer for 4 minutes.
9. Turn hamburgers and set timer for another 4 minutes.
10. Carefully remove pan from the oven (be sure to use hot pads) and place on wire rack.

TO ASSEMBLE EACH HAMBURGER:
1. Place lettuce on top half of buns.
2. Add hamburger, 1 tomato slice and 3 pickle slices.
3. Cover with the bottom of the bun halves.

To make each face: (follow picture, page 34)
1. Use two pimiento slices for eyebrows, two dried apricots and two raisins for the eyes.
2. Put radish piece for nose and one gherkin half for the mouth.

6 burgers

ICE CREAM WITCHES

YOU WILL NEED:

2 plastic bags
shallow tray
dinner knife
ice-cream scoop

6 paper muffin baking cups
can opener
measuring spoons
cutting board

INGREDIENTS:

¼ cup shredded coconut
  Green food coloring
  Blue food coloring
6 canned apricot halves
2 red licorice sticks

1 quart vanilla ice cream
12 semisweet chocolate chips
6 candy corns
6 sugar cones

STEPS TO FOLLOW:

1. In plastic bag put 2 tablespoons coconut and 2 to 3 drops green food coloring.
2. Shake well until all coconut is colored.
3. Repeat with the rest of the coconut and blue coloring.
4. Cut each apricot half into two pieces with dinner knife.
5. Cut licorice into 1½-inch pieces with dinner knife.

To make one Witch:

1. Scoop ice cream into paper muffin cup.
2. Decorate as in the picture by using coconut and two apricot pieces for the hair.
3. Use two chocolate chips for eyes and candy corn for the nose.
4. Put one piece licorice for the mouth and top with sugar cone for the hat.
5. Repeat making 5 more Witches.
6. Place on shallow tray and freeze.

6 Witches

CRANNY SHAKE

YOU WILL NEED:

liquid measuring cup
electric blender or electric mixer
4 tall drinking glasses

INGREDIENTS:

2 cups milk
2 cups (1 pint) orange sherbet
1 cup cranberry juice

BEFORE YOU START: Ask adult to show you how to use electric blender.

STEPS TO FOLLOW:

1. Measure milk and sherbet into blender.
2. Cover and blend on medium speed one minute.
3. Pour in cranberry juice; blend at low speed. (If you do not have a blender, place ingredients into a bowl and beat well with electric mixer.)
4. Pour into tall glasses and serve right away.

4 servings

Pictured Opposite
Ice Cream Witches
Hobgoblin Burgers, 33
Hot Crabby Punch, 37

TIC-TAC-TOE PIZZA

YOU WILL NEED:

large frying pan with lid
wooden spoon
measuring spoons
large mixing bowl
rubber spatula

knife
cutting board
pot holders
jelly roll pan

INGREDIENTS:

1 13¾-ounce package hot roll mix
1 teaspoon vegetable oil
1 pound ground beef
1 envelope dry onion-mushroom mix
1 15-ounce can tomato sauce

½ teaspoon oregano
1½ cups (6 ounces)
   shredded pizza cheese
1 3½-ounce package sliced pepperoni
1 green pepper, cut into strips
1 tomato, cut into slices

BEFORE YOU START: Preheat oven to 425°. Grease 15 x 10 x 1-inch jelly roll pan. Have adult help you slice a green pepper into strips and a tomato into thin slices.

STEPS TO FOLLOW:

1. Prepare hot roll mix following package directions for pizza dough.
2. Use vegetable oil to grease fingers and pat dough into jelly roll pan, going up to ½ inch on the sides.
3. Place in preheated 425° oven and set timer for 15 minutes.
4. Meanwhile, place meat in frying pan over medium heat.
5. Cook until browned, using wooden spoon to break up the meat.
6. Have adult help you drain off the fat.
7. Stir in onion-mushroom mix, tomato sauce and oregano.
8. Cover and simmer 10 minutes.
9. Remove pizza crust from oven.
10. Carefully spread meat mixture over the baked crust.
11. Sprinkle with cheese.
12. Use pepperoni slices to form tic-tac-toe board. (As in the picture.)
13. Use green pepper strips and tomato slices for "X" and "O."
14. Place back in the 425° oven for 10 more minutes.

12 servings

Tic-Tac-Toe Pizza

HOT CRABBY PUNCH

YOU WILL NEED:
3-quart saucepan
liquid and dry measuring cups
measuring spoons
wooden spoon
slotted spoon

INGREDIENTS:
5 cups sweet apple cider
4 cups cranberry juice cocktail
¼ cup firmly packed light
   brown sugar

1 cinnamon stick
½ teaspoon whole allspice
½ teaspoon whole cloves
   Apple slices and
   cinnamon for garnish

STEPS TO FOLLOW:
1. Measure cider, cranberry juice cocktail, brown sugar, cinnamon stick, allspice and cloves into 3-quart saucepan.
2. Place over medium-high heat and bring to a boil. (Do not cover pan.)
3. When punch begins to boil, turn heat to low and simmer 20 minutes.
4. With slotted spoon, remove spices before serving.
5. Decorate with apple slices and cinnamon sticks if you like.

About 9 cups or
12 ¾-cup servings

EASTER PARTY

BUTTERSCOTCH CANDY DROPS

YOU WILL NEED:
medium saucepan
rubber spatula
teaspoon
24 miniature crinkled paper cups
cookie sheet

INGREDIENTS:
1 6-ounce package butterscotch chips
2 tablespoons crunchy peanut butter
¼ cup quick or old-fashioned oats
½ cup bran flakes

STEPS TO FOLLOW:
1. Put butterscotch chips, peanut butter, oats and bran flakes in saucepan.
2. Place on burner and turn the heat to low.
3. Mix together, using a rubber spatula, until all ingredients are melted.
4. Arrange paper cups on cookie sheet.
5. Drop one rounded teaspoon of butterscotch mixture into paper cups.
6. Place cookie sheet in the refrigerator until drops are firm, about 2 to 3 hours.

About 2 dozen drops

CURRANT JELLY PUNCH

YOU WILL NEED:
1-quart saucepan
liquid and dry
   measuring cups
knife
medium mixing bowl

lemon juice squeezer
egg beater
wooden spoon
wooden board
2-quart pitcher

INGREDIENTS:
2 cups water
1 10-ounce jar
   currant jelly
2 oranges

3 lemons
¼ cup sugar
1 quart ginger ale, chilled

STEPS TO FOLLOW:
1. Measure water into saucepan and bring to boil over high heat.
2. Pour 1 cup of the boiling water into mixing bowl. Add jelly.
3. Beat well with egg beater.
4. Add remaining water to dissolve the jelly.
5. Stir in the sugar and place in the refrigerator until cold, about 1 hour.
6. Ask adult to help you cut oranges and lemons in half. Squeeze them to get the juice. Add both lemon and orange juices to the jelly mixture.
7. Place in refrigerator until ready to serve.
8. Just before serving, add the chilled ginger ale and stir.

About 2 quarts punch

Pictured Opposite
Very Special Easter Eggs, 40

VERY SPECIAL EASTER EGGS

YOU WILL NEED:

medium and small
  mixing bowls
wooden spoon
liquid measuring cup
empty egg carton

large needle
container with cover
  for storing
small saucepan

INGREDIENTS:

  6 large eggs
  2 envelopes unflavored gelatin
  1 3-ounce package fruit-flavored gelatin
1½ cups water

STEPS TO FOLLOW:

1. To prepare egg shells: use a large needle and pierce the wide end of the egg. Tap with the needle to make a hole one-half inch wide.
2. Stick the needle into the egg to break the yolk.
3. Hold the egg over a small bowl and shake to allow the inside to run out the hole.
4. Carefully run water inside the shell and let it run back out. Let eggshell dry thoroughly, about 30 minutes.
5. Put the eggs that you have emptied from the shells into a clean container and cover. Store in the refrigerator.
6. Measure water into small saucepan. Place over high heat to boil.
7. Combine unflavored gelatin and fruit-flavored gelatin in mixing bowl.
8. Add boiling water and stir with a wooden spoon until all the gelatin is dissolved.
9. Set aside to cool 10 minutes.
10. Then pour part of the gelatin mixture into a one-cup liquid measuring cup.
11. Hold each eggshell carefully in your hand and slowly pour the gelatin mixture into the dry eggshells.
12. Place the filled egg with the hole on top in the egg carton.
13. When you have filled all the eggs, carefully place the carton in the refrigerator and chill until firm, 5 hours or overnight. *TO PEEL THE EGGS:* Remove the outer shell first, then the membrane. (This is the thin skin inside the shell.) If you find it hard to peel, *quickly* dip the chilled egg (with the shell) into a bowl of warm water before you start to peel. You will find the membrane peels off very easily.

6 eggs

KIDDIE CONES

AMBROSIA CONES

YOU WILL NEED:

medium mixing bowl
can opener
dinner knife

rubber spatula
strainer
measuring spoons

INGREDIENTS:

1 8-ounce can pineapple chunks
1 11-ounce can mandarin oranges
2 bananas
1 cup miniature marshmallows

¼ cup coconut
½ cup non-dairy whipped topping
6 flat-bottom ice-cream cones
4 whole maraschino cherries

STEPS TO FOLLOW:

1. Drain pineapple and mandarin oranges.
2. Place the fruit into the bowl.
3. Slice bananas into bowl.
4. Add marshmallows, coconut and whipped topping.
5. Gently mix to coat the fruit with the whipped topping.
6. Place in the refrigerator to chill 1 hour before serving.
7. To serve, spoon filling into each ice-cream cone until heaping full.
8. Decorate with a whole cherry.

6 cones

ORANGE-VANILLA CONES

YOU WILL NEED:

medium saucepan
liquid measuring cup
wooden spoon
large metal spoon

INGREDIENTS:

1 3½-ounce package
   vanilla pudding mix
1¾ cups milk
2 orange slices

¼ cup frozen orange juice
   thawed and undiluted
6 flat-bottom
   ice-cream cones

STEPS TO FOLLOW:

1. Empty dry pudding mix into the saucepan.
2. Stir in milk, using the wooden spoon.
3. Place over low heat.
4. Stir until the mixture bubbles and comes to a boil.
5. Remove from the heat and stir in the orange juice.
6. Put in the refrigerator to chill about 3 hours.
7. Remove from the refrigerator.
8. Spoon into each ice-cream cone until heaping.
9. To decorate, have adult cut two orange slices into four parts.
10. Place one part orange slice on top of each cone.

6 cones

Easter Bunny Cake

EASTER BUNNY CAKE

YOU WILL NEED:

electric mixer with large
  and small bowls
2 nine-inch cake pans
liquid and dry
  measuring cups
rubber and metal spatulas

cutting board
knife
wire racks
pot holders

INGREDIENTS:

1 18¾-ounce package
  yellow cake mix
1 7-ounce package fluffy
  white frosting mix
1⅓ cups flaked coconut

Red food coloring
Small colored gumdrops
Black shoestring licorice

BEFORE YOU START: Have adult show you how to use electric mixer. Grease and flour two 9-inch round cake pans.

STEPS TO FOLLOW:

1. Prepare cake mix following package directions but bake in two 9-inch cake pans. Cool.
2. Cut one cake layer as shown in the diagram. Leave the other layer whole.
3. Tint ¼ cup coconut pink using a couple drops of red food coloring. Set this coconut aside for the inside of the bunny's ears.
4. Prepare frosting mix following package directions.
5. Arrange cake as shown in the diagram, using the frosting to hold the pieces together.
6. Frost the entire cake.
7. Sprinkle with white coconut and decorate with licorice and gumdrops to make the face and collar. (See the picture.)
8. Use pink coconut to make the inside of the ears.

1 Bunny Cake

SLUMBER PARTY

GUMDROP DELIGHT

YOU WILL NEED:

ice-cream scoop
scissors
liquid measuring cup

large tablespoon
tall drinking glass
wooden toothpicks

INGREDIENTS:

2 scoops soft strawberry ice cream
4 small gumdrops
¾ cup milk
½ cup strawberry soda drink
   Whole gumdrops, whipped cream or animal cookies for garnish

STEPS TO FOLLOW:

1. Place one scoop of ice cream in a tall glass.
2. With scissors, cut up the gumdrops and stir half into the ice cream in the glass.
3. Pour in the milk and soda.
4. Top with the other scoop of ice cream and the rest of the cut-up gumdrops.
5. Garnish with gumdrop figures, whipped cream or animal cookies.
6. To make gumdrop figures, put gumdrops together with toothpicks.

one 12-ounce serving

SPARKLING APPLE JUICE

YOU WILL NEED:

knife
cutting board
2-quart pitcher

INGREDIENTS:

1 quart (4 cups) apple juice
3 thin slices orange, cut in half
3 thin slices lemon, cut in half
   10-ounce bottle ginger ale, chilled
   Ice cubes

BEFORE YOU START: Have adult help you cut orange and lemon slices.

STEPS TO FOLLOW:

1. Pour apple juice into pitcher.
2. Add orange and lemon slices and place in refrigerator until ready to serve.
3. Just before serving add chilled ginger ale.
4. To serve, place 2 ice cubes in each glass before pouring in apple juice.
5. Add an orange and lemon slice to each glass.

4 to 6 servings

Ice Cream Nosegay
Ice Cream Sandwich
Ice Cream Flower Pots
Ice Cream Cart

ICE CREAM NOSEGAY

YOU WILL NEED:
regular-size fluted baking cups
small paper lace doilies
ice cream scoop

INGREDIENTS:
Ice cream
Round peppermint candies
Cinnamon candies

STEPS TO FOLLOW:
1. Fit one fluted baking cup into a second one for each ice-cream nosegay.
2. Place a scoop of ice cream in each double baking cup.
3. Stand round peppermint candies up around the edge of the ice cream (as in the picture).
4. Put cinnamon candies on the top.
5. Place a paper doilie under each ice cream nosegay.
6. Serve right away or freeze until ready to serve.

44

ICE CREAM SANDWICH

YOU WILL NEED:
knife
cutting board

INGREDIENTS:
1 pint of brick ice cream (½ gallon size would be too large)
8 graham crackers
   Chocolate sprinkles
   Candy dots

BEFORE YOU START: Have adult help you cut ice cream into 4 equal slices.

STEPS TO FOLLOW:
1. Place a slice of ice cream between two graham crackers, making a sandwich.
2. Dip sandwich sides into chocolate sprinkles or candy dots.
3. Serve right away or freeze until ready to serve.

4 Ice Cream Sandwiches

ICE CREAM FLOWER POTS

YOU WILL NEED:
6 ¾-ounce heavy paper cups with handles
ice cream scoop

INGREDIENTS:
Ice cream
Small candy suckers
Mint leaf gumdrop candies

STEPS TO FOLLOW:
1. Fill a paper cup with scoops of ice cream.
2. Put a candy sucker in the center of the top scoop of ice cream.
3. Stand candy leaves (as in the picture) upright on both sides of the sucker.
4. Serve right away or freeze until ready to serve.

ICE CREAM CART

YOU WILL NEED:
knife
cutting board

INGREDIENTS:
 1 pint brick ice cream
 8 animal cookies
16 gingersnaps or vanilla wafers

BEFORE YOU START: Place 4 small plates in the refrigerator to chill. Have adult help you cut ice cream into 4 equal slices.

STEPS TO FOLLOW:
1. Place each ice cream slice on a chilled plate.
2. Stand 2 animal cookies up in front of each ice cream slice.
3. Make "wheels" along both sides of ice cream slices with the cookies.
4. Serve right away or freeze until ready to serve.

4 Ice Cream Carts

Baked Beans
Tasty Hamburgers, 47
Sparkling Apple Juice, 43

BAKED BEANS

YOU WILL NEED:
wooden spoon
pot holders
rubber spatula
1-quart casserole dish
measuring spoons
dry measuring cups

INGREDIENTS:
2 1-pound cans baked beans
¼ cup chili sauce
1 tablespoon instant minced onion
2 tablespoons brown sugar

BEFORE YOU START: Preheat oven to 375°.

STEPS TO FOLLOW:
1. Measure all ingredients into a mixing bowl.
2. Mix well.
3. Pour into casserole dish.
4. Place in preheated 375° oven and set timer for 30 minutes.

6 servings

TASTY HAMBURGERS

YOU WILL NEED:

large mixing bowl
measuring spoons
dry measuring cups

fork
large frying pan
pancake turner

INGREDIENTS:

2 pounds ground beef
1/3 cup drained pickle relish
1 tablespoon prepared mustard
1 teaspoon salt

1/2 teaspoon pepper
2 tablespoons margarine
6 hamburger buns

STEPS TO FOLLOW:

1. Put ground beef, pickle relish, mustard, salt and pepper into mixing bowl.
2. Mix thoroughly, using a fork.
3. Shape into 6 patties, about 3 inches round and 1 inch thick.
4. Place margarine in frying pan and set over medium heat to melt.
5. Fry hamburgers for about 10 minutes. Turn often using a pancake turner.
6. Serve on hamburger buns.

6 servings

NO-BAKE CHOCOLATE BALLS

YOU WILL NEED:

large mixing bowl
wooden spoon
liquid and dry measuring cups
jelly roll pan

rolling pin
waxed paper
small saucepan
rubber spatula

INGREDIENTS:

2 8½-ounce boxes chocolate wafers
¼ cup (½ stick) butter or margarine
1 cup confectioners' sugar
1/3 cup frozen orange juice, thawed and undiluted
¼ cup light corn syrup
1 cup finely chopped walnuts

STEPS TO FOLLOW:

1. Place chocolate wafers between two pieces of waxed paper. Roll a rolling pin over the waxed paper, crushing the wafers.
2. Place crumbs in the mixing bowl.
3. Measure butter into small saucepan and melt over low heat.
4. Pour butter over crushed wafers.
5. Add confectioners' sugar, orange juice, corn syrup and walnuts.
6. Mix together all the ingredients.
7. Shape into 1-inch balls and put on jelly roll pan.
8. Place balls in the refrigerator to chill, at least 2 hours.
9. Roll in confectioners' sugar before serving.

4 dozen cookies

ABOUT THE AUTHOR

Sophie Kay is a vivacious television personality and nationally recognized home economist. She was hostess-emcee of a daily cooking show on WGN-TV in Chicago and is currently doing a cooking segment on WISN-TV in Milwaukee. Throughout the country, Sophie has lectured and conducted many cooking schools for television, radio, newspapers, women's clubs, church and social groups, grade schools, high schools and colleges. She appeals to cooking enthusiasts from all walks of life. Sophie Kay is a graduate of Northwestern University and is a member of American Federation of Radio and TV Artists, American Home Economics Association, Wisconsin Home Economists in Business, Theta Sigma Phi, Alpha Xi Delta and is listed in *Who's Who of American Women.*

Editorial Director, James Kuse
Managing Editor, Ralph Luedtke
Production Editor/Manager, Richard Lawson
Photographic Editor, Gerald Koser
Copy Editor, Norma Barnes

illustrations by

Bill Sanders

designed by

Michele Arrieh

Cover Photo
One-Bowl Chocolate Cake, 12
Chocolate-Chip Cookies, 31